I am
RAMTHA

RAMTHA

AUTHOR
RAMTHA

EDITORS
Cindy Black
Richard Cohn
Greg Simmons
Wes Wait

DESIGNER
Wes Wait
with support & love from Cindy, Greg & Richard

BEYOND WORDS PUBLISHING
P.O. Box 2097
Portland, OR 97208-2097
(503) 228-0910

First United States edition published
by Beyond Words Publishing
Company.

ISBN: 0-89610-004-9
Library of Congress Catalog Card
Number 86-70844

Printed May 1986,

Printed by Mandarin Offset Marketing (H.K.) Ltd

TO THE I AM THAT WE ALL ARE

We published this book for what mattered most to us: for the challenge to do something as outrageous as the subject; to bring to the viewer a phenomenon that defied logic; to touch people's lives; and for the joy.

Since we first met Ramtha our lives have not been the same. At one point in this publishing adventure, I found myself in a forest because Ramtha had suggested that I go out and hug a tree. With my arms around a 100' fir tree, I was looking covertly about to see if anyone was watching. Only the trees were watching. When I got past my embarrassment, I realized I could feel the energy flowing through my arms and my chest, the energy of the earth, as the tree and I were one.

At another point, I found myself exhausted and cold at 18,000 feet near the Mt. Everest base camp in Nepal. My heart started hurting and my left arm went numb. Sitting up kept the pain under control, and I told myself if I could stay awake all night, I would be alive come morning. At dawn, I remembered something Ramtha said, that the soul lives forever, that death is an illusion. I smiled, let go of my fears, and walked out into strong sunlight on snow, pain-free and alive in a new way.

When I asked Wes Wait about designing I Am Ramtha, he said he could only trust his instincts to come up with the design when he had the text and the pictures, in the moment. In short, like Ramtha, he was willing to let it happen. In what follows, you can see for yourself the positive results of that kind of approach.

At the Burklyn Business School, where my wife Cindy and I met, the director, Greg Simmons, had always maintained that successful business required unlimited thinking, and living with integrity. Greg had also been the person who introduced us to Ramtha. So it was only natural that we call upon him in developing this publishing venture. In some of the outrageous and flabbergasting moments that you will encounter in I Am Ramtha, Greg's mark is there quietly between the lines.

My wife Cindy has done everything from handling the computerized manuscript for this book to contributing in significant ways to the design. She has had the honesty to see that emotions form the basic stuff of Ramtha and us all. Ramtha once advised me to observe my good fortune in having such a life's companion. He said of Cindy, "In my time there were not rubies enough to acquire a woman of your beauty." The glimmer of such rubies appears here in this book as well.

Dr. Steven Weinberg probably knows Ramtha as well as anyone can, as his own book Ramtha demonstrates. For his critical role in editing Ramtha's text and for his generous responses each time we called on him, we are grateful.

For their investments of self which go far beyond their contributions of talent and capital, we are grateful as well to the photographer, and our investors.

We wish the reader the same kind of openness that Ramtha and the publication of this book brought to us.

Suddenly your life has turned the corner and there's no going back. It happened that way to JZ Knight, a housewife and mother, living quietly in a home near Tacoma, Washington, about two o'clock on a Sunday afternoon. She and her husband were joking in the living room when what JZ describes as a being of light appeared in the doorway and spoke to her. If something like this were to happen, you'd think it would be in a moment of solitude, or meditation, or spiritual ecstasy. But in this otherwise ordinary moment, she could see and hear what was there.

From that point on JZ became the channel for a 35,000-year-old being who is now a regular part of her life. Since that day she has acted as a channel for his communications to over 10,000 people, has appeared on national television, and has allowed her life to undergo an amazing transformation each time Ramtha appears.

In her role as channel for Ramtha, JZ Knight has touched the lives of people with knowledge of their personal lives, insight, and grasp of the future—all on a level of spirituality and love that are undeniable for those who have witnessed it. One of those who has witnessed this transformation often is Anne-Marie Bennstrom, close friend of JZ Knight.

The Publisher

The winds of change upon this plane have brought into focus thoughts and events that have challenged the mind to press forward into a totally new world of possibilities. Once we are outside the box of limited thought, the words we have heard for so long become real. If you can think it, you can know it. If you can dream it, you can own it.

Every thought allowed to go the distance of its grandest possibilities becomes, in its collective embrace, that which we term "the Aquarian Age," "the great shift of consciousness," "the new horizon," or whatever we call this magnificent time and space we occupy in the here and now. That Ramtha the Enlightened One has chosen to appear at this particular time in our history cuts, by his very presence, to the core of our rigid, fear-packed thought capsule, the only world we have known for so long.

"You, my beloved brethren, are the cause of your creation, all of it. It is your own dream you are living, it is your own reality you are acting out on this stage of life. How will you come to know all there is to know? Accept what you are, take responsibility for all you have created. Love yourself. Feel joy and allow, allow, allow!!"

From where comes the power of Ramtha's words; from where spring the emotions that bring rivulets of tears from those who hear him? They are the direct response from that greater light that can, with a single word, or a silent gaze, cut through the forgotten and rekindle the flame of a soul, a soul that knows it all and caused it all, and now, heavy with wisdom, is ready to make the trek back home.

The fact that Ramtha has chosen not to embody and instead to express his strong, masculine, all-powerful energy through a delightful and very feminine vehicle is only one of the wonderful paradoxes we should expect from this unlimited being.

As Ramtha has put it, "I have no face for you to look upon, nor a body for you to worship. I am the Lord of the Wind. If you desire to meet me, go out of your hovels and call me. I will be there. You will feel me like strong fingers through your hair or as a gentle summer breeze caressing your cheek."

JZ Knight, the channel of Ramtha, whom he calls his beloved daughter, fills in every way the awesome role of bringing this great teacher and lover-of-mankind into this dimension. From her initial reaction of fear, doubt, and uncertainty about her own state of mind, she has come to love the Ram and to integrate herself totally with his mind and purpose. After having vacated her body to Ramtha, her first reaction when returning to consciousness is always, "How was it?" "Did everyone like it?" "Do you think they understood?" "Tell me all about it." These simple concerns from JZ may seem incongruous, after she has left an audience spellbound, uplifted, and touched to tears, yet they speak of the natural concerns of the woman who is the channel, who has no awareness of what has happened during Ramtha's appearance. They speak as well of her own involvement with Ramtha's message and her love for the Teacher that once, long ago, was the Father her soul remembered and with whom she always longed to reunite.

JZ has as many facets to her nature as a diamond refracted by the rays of the sun. She can shift from a little girl into a wise sage in a blink of an eye. She calls herself simple but contains a depth and a human capacity that at times are incomprehensible. She is incapable of hiding her feelings behind any social mask. Whatever she feels, she is—and every part of her being reflects it.

It has been my great privilege to watch JZ's personal unfolding ever since the coming of the Ram. The walls of fears and limitations are crumbling around her, and she is rapidly stepping into the sunlight of all her possibilities. She meets the challenge that goes with being the channel for Ramtha with a zestful joy much like that of Ramtha himself. Ramtha says, "I am an outrageous God. I will be what you call fashionable. I love this place and I have come to make a difference."

Whatever goes for Ramtha, so it is for JZ. The world is their playpen. They march to the same tune and are gathering an army behind them, an army with no heavy boots or solemn faces. There is a buoyancy and a joy, a laughter that approaches roaring thunder. We know from Ramtha that ultimately there are no leaders and no followers. It is mankind who, by the touch of a wise and grand master dressed in the delicate body of a woman, has rediscovered God within and is returning back home.

Anne-Marie Bennstrom

Who be I? I am a notorious entity. I have that which is called a reputation. Know you what that is? Controversial, and I do what I say I do. What I am here to do is not to change people's minds, only to engage them and allow the wonderments for those that desire them to come to pass. I have been you and I have become the other side of what you are. So I am your brother. If you haven't become man, you never become Christ, and if you have never become man you

The greatest and most important reason that I am here and you are here is to learn who you are and what you are. What you are is God and once you have embraced that, you have embraced love and when you know love, you become a Christ and when you become a Christ, you become a light unto the whole of the world. When the light shines forth, the consciousness is raised and when the consciousness is raised, it eases into super-consciousness and when superconsciousness is upon the land, that which is called survival, decadence of mind, body and spirit, war and

have not lived in all the kingdoms of God the Father. Becoming man is the epic discovery. No one has allowed you to know yourself, to love yourself, to break through social conscious mind into unlimited thinking. To feel and to know without the uttering of a word. To gain the wisdom, through experience, to understand and go beyond limitation. For when you leave my audience, all you have is you.

pestilence, they are no more. It is finished. God is. That is what you will learn and embrace through profound experience.

When I say to you that I shall teach you to become God, who indeed, do you think you are to become? A pious creature in long robes who can manifest trinkets in his hands? You are simply to become yourself, for where else is the glory of

One who unfolds into his Godhood is one who unfolds into Selfhood. To live as God and to be as God is, is to be as you, to live as you, and to see yourself in all other peoples; to love them and to allow them the same freedom to be and to live as the Father within you has allowed your own supreme and divine self.

God but in the beauty that you are. And where do you go to become yourself? Not to a cave or tall mountain or some forgotten temple. You go within yourself—beyond the illusions of the flesh to the sublime thought and emotion that created the wonderful body that you inhabit so that God could experience the form called humanity.

A God that unfolds is an entity who can look into the eyes of all entities and see within them his own perfect reflection. God realized in self is God seen in all people, all things, all life. To live as God is not at all an arduous thing to do. It is simply breaking away from old habits and formulating new

Living this premise of being God does not mean that you have to be anything other than what you are—without judgment, without fear, without worry, and in all of your acts, put forth joy. You will still retain your unique vigor, your beauty, your integrity, and your style; that shall never be lost. The only difference is that you are recognizing the genius of unlimitedness in your being, rather than the illusions of limitedness that have blinded humanity for eons.

ones. It is getting into the habit of seeing yourself as unlimited God rather than vulnerable man. It is getting into the habit of allowing life to be instead of judging it. It is getting into the habit of laughing instead of worrying. It is getting into the habit of seeing the purposeful good in all things instead of the fault in all things.

Those who are unfolding into their Godhood are finding that life is taking on the glimmer of simplicity rather than complexity. For in being God, no longer does one have to compete for the idyllic, simplistic, unique being; he only has to be. No longer does he have to be like all other peoples; he only has to be himself.

To be as God is, is to worship no thing save you, to love no thing greater than you, to hold no thing more divine than you, and to allow self to be, for that is how the Father is in his supreme state of being.

Learn to be an entity of great humility when it comes to you.
And when moment by moment you give in to the love of self
and allow it to bloom forth, the glory of the kingdom of
Heaven will become prevalent before you. Joy is the magic that
allows it to occur.

I know that for long periods of time your teachers have
intimated that there was more to you than meets the eye.
There is. You don't even know how powerful you are! You
don't reckon at that which is termed the divineness of your
being. If you did, you shan't curse it in the ways that you do,
or make it be the things that it is not prepared to be.
You are more than a man or a woman. You are the creator
of them.

You are God, and I bring forth from that which be I a truth, not a philosophy, and awaken within you latent remembrances for the soul to bring from its surface ancient knowledge that remembers how great it is. Then, woe unto this plane of limited consciousness, for when God is awakened from its slumber, alas, there come forth changes that abound to the greatness of this place and you. In that small understanding it is necessary to grow, but it

The power to emerge as a capable entity of mind and body and spirit, that the whole of that which you are has the capacity to unite itself to transcend the simple need of survival; to know what you have never known; to embrace a feeling that you have never felt; to see beyond the eye what is the unseen; to dream the dream and become the reality; to have the power to heal the body, to heal the spirit; the power to create direction; the power to be without the need of mercy. Now, what of all your wrongs that you have done, and all of your thoughts and all of your plots and plans? Think I think less of you? I do not, for all of your thoughts are purposeful in intent and were supposed to be that way. I do not judge

must be cultivated. You will learn to cultivate your power; not the power to rule the world, or to rule the universe, but the power to possess all kingdoms, without the result of them possessing you. To have the power to make direction in your life; the power to clothe yourself, to give you sustenance— what is called survival. But the power transcends survival.

you; I love you. I love you, for the moment of your damnation is fleeting, my beloved entities, and the moment of your enlightenment is but a moment away, and I know that. Thus, unto you, I shan't teach you that which is termed laws and regulations, for I do not wish to enslave you; I wish to bring you forward to be what you are. And in these teachings, why I am here is to bring forth that memory of that latent God that can come to the surface and see the limitations it has lived in and do something about it. In many ways you have lost that which is termed the remembrance of the dignity of your soul and the enlightenment of your spirit through the grappling for survival here. I have come here to bring you from your cloistered selves back into your knowingness selves, and not with words that beseech the soul to humility and to godly acts, but with teachings that ring forth truth blatantly within the soul, that the soul urges itself to become the divine principle it forgot long, long ago.

You have had many entities come to you, not only in this life but in what is termed your history, that have tried many different avenues to teach you over and over again who you are. And, at most times, they have intervened, not only on your behalf, but for the whole of the world and its cellular existence. But one by one, you have taken them and made

If you gain nothing else here, never stop loving yourself, caring about you and wanting to understand you better, thus enabling a greater peace for you and an understanding of who the Father is in relationship to you. The times that are coming upon this plane are nigh at your door. And they are going to need entities that are strong in their knowingness and in who and what they are.

statues of them. You have twisted and perverted their words according to your own desires and for the purposeful enslavement of other entities. And you have not heard the word. In this that I do, it is wondrous, indeed, for that which I give unto you is a voice, indeed, an even eye, indeed, and that which is termed complete love, for you are loved. Without the face, without the temple, without the feet, without all of the things that you cling to, I'm going to teach you as an illusion that you yourself are.

Do not always try to look behind the curtain of what is entertaining you on the stage. If you are to carry forth a truth no matter what illusion or enigma or pretense it comes in, it is best to be the observer of it and not look for whys or how comes. For when you do that, you get lost in the murk and the mire and lose the affect of the illusion. It does not matter who and what I am, it is the fact that I work—better than anything you know.

Know you why I do not appear as I am? For I do not wish to be the ideal in physical understanding. You are the ideal, right within you. Now it is certain that I am who I am, for my daughtren, indeed, is what is termed a lady in your terms and be not this way at all in her own personality form of existence. And as she be liken unto the lot of you, she also is learning and allowing and becoming. But when I leave you there is no image to worship. There are no feet to bow down to. There is no picture of me to hang around your necks. And you can't follow me where I go, for you have not learned the art of being wholly divine—but you will.
There are multitudinous books written on how to become enlightened. Most have not begun to describe the word enlightenment. They use it without understanding what it is. It means to be in knowledge of.

That understanding of enlightenment must first begin with you. When the feeling can be touched and the soul can be opened, miracles can be worked. And they are always worked in the wonderment and for the glory of God that lives within you. But if you do not look within and begin therein, wonderments shan't exist for you, only words, only the pursuit of idle promises given to fool yourself.

I want you to know what is spoken, is. And for you in your life, that is all that is important—not beliefs of religions or hierarchies, but truth. And live that to the greatest example that your being can live.

I shan't be worshipped. I shan't be ridiculed for. That is not needed. I am a warrior, indeed! I am a God who hath acclaimed himself by doing! And that which I teach you I will teach you by doing. And all changes that come forth are for the adventure, the adventure of experiencing a greater and more lofty unlimitedness. And if this now changes in the nows that are yet to be born, so be it, for that makes up the fundamental self that is called God. You are an entity energy that has consummated itself into mass and matter. What you feel this moment may change the next. Understanding that you are a God that has such options, is one who can love himself in freedom to exercise those options.

I will be with you forever, for my reach goes into forever, for I am not the limitation of an embodiment. I am indeed the collectiveness of this thought synthesis that I am teaching you of. I will be with each of you. All you have to do is ponder me and I will help you.

My conquest was not with nations, but with I, Ramtha. And I bloomed into Ramtha, the Enlightened One, when I found who be I unto the mystery called myself. I will teach you how to look at yourself evenly and to know who you are and what you are; and to have the forthrightness to invite change and embark upon its wondrous path.

I am here to teach you of a God that is simple and pure and omnipresent, wherever you are. That doesn't mean you have to do anything different except realize that the grandest temple of all you are; and that your life is all that is important— not the rules and regulations of someone else, but the sincere freedom to express your divine self.

I am hard to believe in. This is a truth. But you never listened any other way. So through this means, be I now. I only want you to be happy and know that the Father approves of you; and that you have to confess nothing except your love of self; that is all. That is all that needs to be learned here. And if anyone wishes to hurt you because of this that you have heard from me, deny me, completely—but remember what I have taught you, because it will happen.

There are many of you who think that because I am not here in this embodiment that I am not here. That is for you to learn. But I have watched you go from soothsayer to soothsayer and teacher to teacher, and I am enamored, indeed, for what you repetitively ask and never are satisfied with.

You are never going to get that which is termed the right answer, ever, for you, until you ask yourself, for only therein lies the answer. Only therein. And for as many of them as there are, they are all going to have a different definition and a different mannerism. But it still will not resolve what is within you.

Do not be caught up in that which is termed fear and running from one entity to another to gain advice. Ask yourself, the Father that is within you. It will give you the peace and the wholeness and the love and the steadfastness which none other can give to you, save yourself.

What greater compliment can any of you give unto your own beauteous self than to say: Who be I unto this moment, indeed, that glorifies and exalts and exudes this moment, be the God-fire of my being that has reached forth and created and seen all things as vivid life unfolding before me. I be God, the creator that recognizes creation, for without me, nothing is.

It takes a rather bold and driven entity to express what they are. And to survive on this plane, it takes one that is arrogant and selfish and is self-adoring—and those are all things that make up the continuity of God. For you to become unlimited, is only to be you, happily, and to live that every moment. Being who you are is being the balance of life and living who you are, so there is no diversion, nor duality in your wisdom. Then you are living a truth, aligned in your being, a light to the world.

It doesn't matter whether you trust God. All that matters is that you trust yourself. The other will inevitably follow. And it is not important whether you believe in God, for you are still here and you're still loved to be whatever you want to be.

It is for you to know that I have always loved you and I have never left you. And though there be those who be separate from this plane, for they are the master of all planes, it is their choosing to be separate. Mine is not. You are my family that I love greatly. You are unto my being the fulfillment that once we did long ago will come into that which is termed an hour of completion.

There are steps into forever. This is one of them. When I'm not here with you, I am also somewhere else with someone else in another level, in another time, another dimension. And they're ongoing. So, our adventure does not cease when you pass this plane; it only begins—and it is ongoing.

We are going to climb the ladder into innerspace. So be it. There shall come an hour, my beloved entities, where the moment which we share shan't be, for I will be no more. And you will have embarked upon a grand destiny, grander than that which you have the capacity within your thinking mind to realize.

All that I have told you, you will hold and remember in the Lord God of your being. And all that is spoken will manifest for the glory of the God, the Father that is in all of you, for these words are here to become. And when leave I, you will have all that you wanted; but what they will teach you is how precious you are to the whole of all life. That is what I am here for. And for such destiny I will teach you well.

I am
NATURE

It was the elements that taught me of God. And the elements never taught me failure, you see, because they are consistent. The sun never cursed me. The moon never said I must be this way. The wind teased me and tantalized me. And the frost and dew, and the smell of grass, and insects going to and fro, and the cry of the night hawk—you know, they are unfailing things; and their science is simple. And the wonderful thing I learned about them is that in their simplicity and steadfastness they utter not one word. The sun did not look down at me and say, "Ramtha, you must worship me in order to know me." And, the sun did not look down at me and say, "Ramtha, wake up. It is time to look upon my beauty!" It was there when I looked to see it.

What is the fourth color of the rainbow? What is the color of poppy? What is the color of the great lights that come from within the earth and shine brilliantly into the sky? And what does soil smell like? And what does a leaf that has just fallen feel like? Where does the secret world of an insect lie? And what of an elf and a dwarf or a fairy? Where, pray tell, have they gone? Are they real? What are the colors of their wings, their noses, their skin, their ears?

And what is it like to embrace a tree that hath never felt the touch of man, to climb a mountain, to breathe a cloud and let it lie lazily upon your being until it is ready to move on; or to live in a cave, to light a fire to warm yourself from cold to heat, to light, to darkness? What does it sound like to hear a wild cat scream in the night or a butterfly when it speaks to a flower?

Who set the lights into the heavens, indeed? Who created another universe that you have not even the eyes to see, and yet more after more after more? Who called forth your waters called your deep, from out of the skies unto this plane? And who created the flower? Not God, the isness, for it is the isness that is the mass that makes up all of these things. It was YOU, my esteemed and beloved brethren, who did all of these things, just as you have created your world as you know it. This is how magnificent you are. Ponder a moment, a fantasy. Think of a fantasy…thrilling, volatile, explosive to your being…and soon you will feel all the feelings of that fantasy. That is how your universe was created.

Unto the Christ, God-man, indeed, am I a lover of, for without that which is termed the Christus, or humanity, the flora shan't bloom, indeed, the seasons shan't be, and the sun would never rise, and the winds would never blow, for man created this kingdom according to that which is termed his purposeful intent desire, and all things have come forth willingly to give credence to the beauty of mankind which so many forget.

When night falls and there is slumber in the air and all is still and quiet and the stars twinkle benevolently in their heaven, and the moon in her journey waxes and wanes all the way until dawn, and there is nothing that you have to live for, or be for, or do for—in the quiet of those moments, entity, you will question your own honor and your own nobility, your own truth, and the quality of your existence. And if your nights are not filled with slumber and peaceful dreams, then perhaps you need to reassess how you are living in the moments of day when you have to live for all the perplexities of everyone else.

A great master comes to be in peace and harmonic attunement with that which is termed the flower—in which everyone finds harmony, because it doesn't dispute them. It doesn't put them in contention. Nor does it, indeed, make them jealous. It simply is. You adore the flower. And you take your air for granted. And your water, it runs endlessly, for "there will always be more."

Everything you are in harmony with…except mankind. And that is where that which is termed all warlords lie, all overtaking, all misery, and all pain. That is your great mastery. A master learns the secret that is very simple: that to love God is to be at peace with ALL THINGS—all things.

The Unknown God allowed the creative mind, which is God-man, to exist. And what is most remarkable is, when war was fought in the west, and the midnight sky was like daylight from the fire, the Enchantress still stayed on her journey; and all of her children, the stars, were still there.

And when the dying in the morning occurred, the great jewel in the heaven, RA, still came up, passive unto the illusions created by God-man. The wildfowl made their sojurn to the rivers, and the flutter of silver wings was still apparent when the struggle for power was occurring below them. And when children laughed, and the wind blew, and old women wept, and old soldiers were weak, the seasons still came and went. Why didn't the moon stop and listen when a conspiracy was on the rise? Why didn't the wildfowl acknowledge the birthing of children, hard pressed by their mother in the early morning? They never acknowledged it.

Do you have the answers to all of these things? Then it is time you did. This is a wondrous experience. This kingdom should never have been missed by anyone, for it gives virtue, beauty and insight to all who experience it.

Without you, the flower does not bloom. Without you, the seasons do not come. Without you, the grains of sand in the sea do not become more and shift with the ebb and flow of the tides. Without you, frost does not become crystalline on a window. Without you, the beauty of a scarlet bird is never acknowledged. All of this kingdom was created by and for you. Remember that.

Love what you are. That is all that is important. Love the God that you are. That is all that is important. Embrace the wind, and the willow, and the water, for it is the creation of your importance. And be at peace, wherever and whatever that is for you.

This hour that we have come unto, the most important of all hours this day, your enchantress, she is already hiding her face amongst the trees. This is the only plane with darkness on it, but it is the only plane with the enchantress, and that is something wonderful.

Your plane will not perish. It will not quake and split and come apart. The oceans will stay where they are. This plane will gracefully move into the ebbs…of another time.

Always you will be in my soul. I love you greatly. March through this life with tender care. And whenever you need to learn greater and to learn more, come into my kingdom. I will meet you here and in the mountains, where one can be exalted. And I will teach and render and manifest for you 'til you can go where I go as I am. So be it.

To walk alone in the forest is to walk unmolested,
To climb the peak of a grand mountain
And feel the wind, icy cold, strong fingers through your hair,
And breathe impeccable breath,
And to see valleys far, far away,
To sit in a stream of running water forever, forever, forever,
To place a thought on a passing leaf as it makes its way to the ocean,
To be filled in the joy of midnight,
To dance like elfin queens underneath starry midnight,
To become intoxicated with the light of the silvery moon
Waxing and waning till dawn,
To be astride a great fiery steed riding with the wind
And having its mane blowing around your chest and in your face
As you cover meadows, hills and dales,
And riding wild and free,
Of being a great seer
Who can see the invisible world dance and play,
Without harm, without violence, without misery.
To go and sit by a crackling fire,
Watching the sparks and the embers glow and hue
Like some faraway city,
To have soft slippers and good tobacco
And the smell of old books and fine leather,
To have a pot of tea, and to sip it,
To look behind you, at the window, curtains drawn alas,
And see the twinkling forever in midnight dancing,
And the moment of that silence only disturbed by the cry of a night bird,
As it wings its way into the dapple wood
And the faintness of it is heard,
And, alas, you watch the embers,
And all that you are,
And all that you are enjoying,
The splendor of that moment impregnated with life,
Brings unsolicited joy that is beyond understanding,
It is simple.

Iam
NOBLE VIRTUE

What anyone can teach you, you can find in the sweet waters of a gentle brook or the glorious blaze at sunset or the wondrous colors at midnight or in the mute beauty of the heavens. Teaching is allowed when one experiences the laughter of a child that is sweet and innocent, the flush upon the cheeks of some beautiful woman, a maiden who realizes her coming womanhood and does not meet your eyes, the breast of some great steed that is stroked kindly.

This life, your life, is your teacher. But you must be a participant in it by living it.

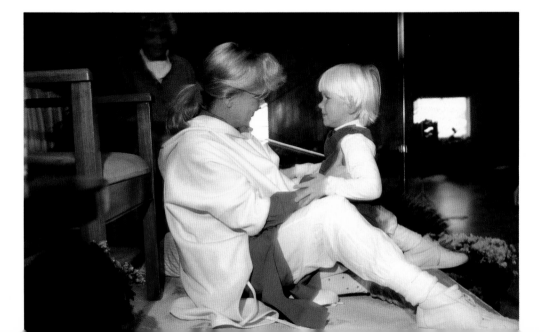

And the feelings will befall you and you will weep when looking at the sun. And you will weep at a child's laughter. You will be humbled by the seasons. And you will hear the blooming of a flower, and you will hear a fish and its movement. You are going to experience feelings as you have never experienced them before. We set them into motion in but a moment, and this lifetime will play it through. And all of the interchange of emotions that you experience will all add to that which is called the noble virtue of your totality.

You have lived millions of lifetimes. This lifetime is but a breath in the great wind. In the dream you come and go. You are born and you die, you live again over and over, and over.

When you have lived all that you are spent on living for society, and when night falls and there is slumber in the air and all is still and quiet, and the stars twinkle benevolently in their heaven, and the moon in her journey waxes and wanes all the way until dawn, and there is nothing that you have to live for or do for—in the quiet of those moments you will question your own honor and your own nobility, your own truth, and the quality of your existence. And if your nights are not filled with slumber and peaceful dreams, then perhaps you need to reassess how you are living in the moments of day when you have to live for all the perplexities of everyone else. Every one of you were virtuous in every life you began. You are rich with the ancient past but are virgins to the present and future.

Live every moment to its fullest measure. Noble virtue is acquired, not by having the abstinence of life, entity, but the full thrust of it. Be patient. You will live forever if you do. And experience everything that is being brought into your life at the moment that it is happening.

To become peaceful is to do away with the facades, the illusions, the images that you wear for everyone and simply be free, wild and wonderful to you. That is all you have to do. And in the processes, you gain virtue and nobility; you see your inner beauty; you find inner peace. Then, if the whole of the world is for you, so be it. If the whole of the world is against you, so be it. For what you have acquired is yourself and the love of that sacred self that lies behind the illusion of the flesh. Nothing can take that from you, ever. Not even the enigma of death can take it from you, for who you are is indeed immortal. But in order to obtain that peace, you must be willing to give up your unhappiness and simply allow yourself to be.

Allow that which is termed the virtue of self to emerge forward and live.

You will be totally glorified to find that you are a great entity, for you never have known such compassion and humility and such greatness; and such that you have within your being that you have only dared to imagine in others, you also possess. And when you touch on each of those wonderful facets of your soul, indeed your spirit, that you take a breath of what is you and see the glory of what I see in each of you, then from that point and measure, and desiredly so, you will see that in others.

Many have tried upon this plane to impart upon you that which is termed noble virtue, to teach you simply of who you are, and you have hated and despised the lot of them. The way humanity is enhanced is when one entity blooms and becomes the vessel of love of self: a noble creature of esteem, knowledge, virtue, compassion and wisdom; that lives unaffected by society, fashion and trends—a virtual hero. Anyone that can sustain beyond social consciousness deserves recognition. One who blooms and loves himself completely, understands himself completely, is volatile to himself, becomes a ''light'' to others.

The one thing despised greater than anything on this plane is noble virtue—and yet it is succored unto by every entity trying to find himself.

It is quite one thing when an entity that has noble virtue, that has experienced all things, says alas, ''I am finished here. There is nigh not one thing that I want. There is not one fine silk I desire. There is not one great mansion or hovel that I want to possess. I have had it all. Now I am free to be one with the wind''.

It is quite another to love yourself and do what you must do within your own being first. And if there be one or a host of entities that love you not for that which you have chosen to do, love them enough to give them the freedom to despise you if they wish. And know and understand within the wisdom of your being that that is their truth; do not try to take it away from them. And then continue to live according to your own virtue, according to your own aims. Then you will be a light unto all people, for you are the God steadfast that is in love and joy with itself, who emanates a radiance of compassion and understanding for everyone. That is the only way that it is ever achieved. It is not hard to do this, it only means living in spite of everyone else. Live through the honor and noble character that is acceptable to you— regardless of what is acceptable to anyone else.

That which you get you need because you want it, because your soul needs it. It does not need it to guild your walls or to cushion your feet; it needs it for the experience of knowing what that feels like. That is a part called cumulative noble virtue.

Absorb as you can so that you are a light to the other parts of the world who are not here. And this labor, I assure you, will reach beyond your children's children. What you learn here will be a way of life for them. And that is a good thing, for they are the means for your advent back to this plane. This humanity will be enlightened beyond the word enlightenment by greater of your brothers; they are swifter, more cunning, more clever, more technically advanced, more mindful, more loving, more brilliant, more wise—a great intimidation for they are

all-noble in their virtue to this plane. And they shall put this mankind in that which is termed a wrothful state. But for a few who know and who understand, they shall be called ``the peacemakers.'' They will inherit this earth for they are simple, indeed, the God within—and they are you.

I am THE TEACHER

I teach on what I know, what I have been, and what I am. And I know of a truth, not a philosophy, that works for all peoples, in however manner they wish to apply it to themselves. This teaching is lawless—it possesses no law!

For law is a limitation; it obstructs freedom. The wind is lawless; it goes where it wishes to go.

The moment I, or any teacher, or any purported lover of mankind sets into a regulated form how man must be in his perfection, he is enslaving man. Man's undoing of himself is trying to be the truth of other men and how they live, rather than how he lives.

As a teacher of your beings, I have been a manifestor unto your beings, for mankind has no great "emotional enigmas" when he prudently sits and listens. Only when he is thrust into the midst of what is being taught does he learn.

And woe, there has been no one on this plane that has demonstrated these teachings liken unto my being, for all can speak the words yet none can manifest them. Each that are gathered here, the word is manifested into a reality to teach, a wondrous way to learn.

The greatest teaching is life and the experience of it, and the rounding of it, and the beauty of it. That brings you to the knowingness; it brings you to the awareness. It brings you to the purposeful being that you are.

And the teacher is always there whenever the student wishes to listen. You are no less than any that have ever been, for the same teacher that exists within them exists within you. That teacher possesses not words; it possesses feelings. Begin to listen to the voice within you. In doing that, you will have all the answers to everything you ever wished to know.

Listen to your feelings. They will tell you where to go. They will teach you how to be. They will teach you how to live.

Thus, unto you, I shan't teach you that which is termed laws and regulations, for I do not wish to enslave you; I wish to bring you forward to be what you are.

Teachers have come and gone on this plane, some wonderfully famous, and some forgettable, and some unforgettable. But it really hasn't caused much of a difference because everyone has lived how they wanted to in the first place.

Humanity will get helped when it wants to get helped. And most of the time, it will turn a deaf ear to anyone who is struggling to do it—and rightfully it should, for who is to say anyone needs help? Only when they ask; that is when they need it. The other times they are doing precisely what they want to do—and that is their state of happiness. You know, this plane is weary of philosophers; it is weary of teachers.

To share with someone else may seem noble at first, but lo, I say to you, it is a most despairing and arduous job and has no rewards. Don't share with anyone; share with you. Don't share; love—you. Become you. It is not necessary for you to prove that you exist to anyone else, only to you. Steadfast before you stands the greatest teacher of all time. You! If you would only go beyond the stubbornness of your altered ego into the sensitive part of your feelings and listen to them, you would encounter a great and awesome teacher. There is no voice that will teach you greater than your own. There is no word written that will teach you greater than your own. You are your own savior; you are your own master; you are your own teacher. For who you are is the open-minded, unlimited, unexplainable Source.

I am
BECOMING

To become is a great learning, for it means to love yourself and to trust yourself enough to take counsel with yourself and to trust what you hear

Learning is not the engagement of hearing yourself chatter; it is the engagement of hearing the words and feeling them within your being. That is true learning, for the feelings then create the reality within which one can exist.

To be a listener is to be a master; the master that gathers enlightenment, and encourages and feeds his own purposeful good and intent; the master that begins to learn; that begins to open; that begins to feel, to take in, to be, to become.

I have taught you to look within your being and feel from your being the God within you, and to listen to what it tells you; and to have the assertiveness to change, regardless of what the world thinks of you, because it is only your life that you are living and only you are responsible for it—no one else is.

What I have taught you has not been words; they have been meanings, complete memory, an emotion that is there everlasting, forever. And when the feeling arises, you will come down from the mountain, and the wind will be nigh at your back, and the exuberance of life will be in you and in your veins as it was in mine. And behold, the prophecy of the great meek, the great humbled strength, the light of the world will be upon the land.

Whatever it is that you desire to know, I will teach you in that which is termed knowledge; and then you will live through the emotional aspects of that knowledge so that it becomes a reality in your being. Then it is no longer what is termed a belief, as it is a reality.

For long periods here on your plane, your people have been urged to believe in things of uncertainty. Well, I shan't ever desire for you to believe in anything; that is conjecturous and oftentimes dangerous. I want you to know them. And knowing them must be a manifestation of the knowledge by which it is completely understood.

All of this reality is a result of dreams, and in order to make anything better, you must dream it first. For action is feeling. You do not have to lift one hand, but only to feel it. Feelings manifest the thought and through that which is termed emotion manifests the matter, gross matter, that which holds the whole plane together.

Your health is only a product of your thinking. All diseasements are a manifested truth in the body because of the inability to cope with stress, with change. Becoming a master is moving beyond stress. Your body will only last as long as you allow it to last. There is one thing you have to do in order to keep it healthy—you have to be happy—all of the time. Even when you are contemplative, you have to have joy in your being.

Allow yourself to bloom, and cease criticizing yourself, and cease struggling for a very futile ideal. Then you will have sublime peace, for every moment you are the ideal of how you are and every moment you are gaining from that. Simply be the beautiful master that you are and allow laughter to come forth. And do away with the things that bring harshness upon your being.

The master no longer embraces from his illusion into gross matter, but takes the illusion inside and lives it through the emotion and resolves it into wisdom. That is why he can sit beside a dusty road while the saffron dust rises in the morning light, and watch the passersby in their fine glint robes, and their immaculate kerchiefs, and their carriages, and never envy them, because he has been them. All he has to do is embrace the sight upon which his eyes follow, and take it into his soul and live it emotionally, and he is finished with it. And yet he has not moved from his pallet.

Simply be. Do not judge anything. Do not say anything is good and never say it is bad. And do not say this is positive or that is negative, for if you say that you are good, then that equates you are also bad, for that is the balance of good. If you say you are positive, that equates that you are negative also, that you have a duality. God is not a duality. He is the perfect alignment of himself.

And what is becoming? To know who and what you are, that you never doubt the steadfastness of yourself e'er again; to learn to meet terms with you and understand who God is. And for those that are still weary and trying to find and play the game of hide and seek with self, you will continue for a while. But I am not a teacher that gives words; I am that which is termed a manifestor. And I will continue to manifest the drawn desire to look within you—until you take your look. So be it.

Iam
PEELING

All that you want is yours. But you must do away with the struggle, the games, the illusions that keep you from getting it. I urge you to peel away each illusion that inhibits the magnificent creature that lies within you so that you can be a light unto the world, for woe unto this plane, this world is going to need some lights.

To live as God is not at all an arduous thing to do. It is simply breaking away from old habits and formulating new ones. It is getting into the habit of seeing yourself as unlimited God rather than vulnerable man. It is getting into the habit of allowing life to be instead of judging it. It is getting into the habit of laughing instead of worrying. It is getting into the habit of seeing the purposeful good in all things instead of the fault in all things.

You are lost in your own enigma of illusions. You must learn to peel them away, to look beyond the fear, the disappointment, the guilt, the comparison of yourself to others, and find that which is worth looking for, that which is glory, that which is divine. I open the doors, give the teaching. I send the runners. I manifest the glory. But it is of no use until at last you are willing to remove these enigmas from yourself that keep you from that splendid creature that is within you all.

And what have you when you get rid of the "blocks" of insecurity and give up the things that cling to you like leeches, that sap your strength from you, and start doing the things that bring you happiness, regardless of what say the world, and allow your life to unfold in front of you? You have that which is termed a king that sits radiantly in his dominion; that dreams the dream of desire and it burns forth into reality; that speaks forth whatever he desires and it comes to manifest.

Those who are unfolding into their Godhood are finding that life is taking on the glimmer of simplicity rather than complexity. For in being God, no longer does one have to compete for the idyllic, simplistic, unique being; he only has to be. No longer does he have to be like all other peoples; he only has to be himself.

And then, once you go in, you'll find it is going very rapidly. And that which is termed pain you will indeed suffer, but what you will suffer is letting go of appendages of identity. That, the lot of you need to do. But it will render you clean, and pure, and unbendable, and completely aligned. This is a process that you need, for you are on the epoch of a new time and great changes that necessitate one to be brilliant, self-centered, fearless, and loving to all that is.

And remember one thing: Do not ever fear anything. There is nothing that has ever been created in that which is termed the totality of God that would ever take life away from you, for if God would have created a greater source to take away your life or your life force, then He would have created it to His own destruction, and He has not done that. There is nothing worth fearing, for there is nothing that will take you away from life—you will always be. Have dominion over everything. Fear makes you succumb to it; then you become the victim. Become a great Lord and in the face of what would fear the masses, do not fear; for your life is assured for eternity. And do not judge anyone, for remember: what you say about them you are saying about yourself; and what you say from the Christ of your being, he will say "So be it" and your judgment will be your judgment.

There are many of you who are clinging to things. You hold onto them tightly for a reason. Let go of them straightaway! There is no thing that is worth holding onto so tightly if it causes you misery. What is worth that? Allow yourself the grace and the humbleness to let it go. Love yourself by allowing it to fall from your being.

Allow yourself to know that what you are within yourself is valuable enough to let go of what inhibits purposeful happiness and joy within your life.

When you weep and know not why you are weeping, it is the soul expressing a feeling that words cannot comply with. When the soul weeps, you are experiencing an expectancy of adventure! The only way the body can express it is through weeping.

The soul weeps, for there is an expected feeling that brings you back into the alignment called "you," God, what you really are. Then, your life will change. It will change, in great emotion. Entities will leave your life and others will come into it. Your labor will change. Every priority will change. And why? For they were priorities attuned to a lesser frequency. That which comes is attuned to a greater one.

And when the laughter is there, laugh—regardless of who laughs around you. Do not look to see if they are in agreement. Who cares! Be who you are, and cherish it and love it and live it. I will redo your entire kingdom, if you but do it.

To peel away the illusions that hide the distinctive God within you takes courage and what is called the wonderful will "want," to want to. That is when I, lover of your being, can tear down walls, to allow you to walk through; can split the universes to have you a better view if you wish. But it does no good unless you want to.

I am UNCONDITIONAL LOVE

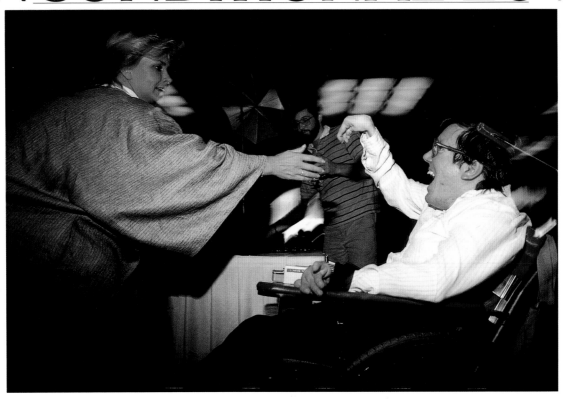

For you, I tell you: You are loved by a seen and an unseen Source that loves what you are, through and through, and that warrants and witnesses your being every moment that you are; and that if all of the world denied who you are and did not love you, master, this Essence, that is the All That Is The All, would be your kingdom.

Why love I you? For unto me you are brethren unto my being. And unto a force that is powerful and unseen, that gives supportive evidence to this your plane, you have great importance. And for you to come into your knowingness as sovereigns rather than dutiful followers, that is the way it should be, and I am the teacher thereof.

Love is an immortal thing—it is what binds us together through the tatters of eons. Though millenniums ago one was lost to one another, the thread of love is quickened when found again and renewed in its vibrancy, for it keeps us together upon this life expanse. Love is the heartbeat of the aqueous. And wherever that is, those that are needing are being drawn to it. The love for you and my peoples has never died and never will. Where I have gone so will you. Love is all you've ever needed to grow and to prosper and to become. That is what I will enrich you and everyone with—that is forever.

Do you know what pure love is? It is love of oneself, the ability of one entity to love himself and to find another entity that is the reflector of his own perfect being that he can love in absolute freedom. Love is not contractual agreements, long-term commitments. If one finds love in a splendid moment, he has found it for the rest of his existence.

The ideal love, entity, is to love someone that reflects all the beauty that you are. And they love you, in turn, because you reflect all that they are; it is soul recognizing itself. And they love you in absolute freedom—it's just that their choice prefers being with you over and above anyone else, for you are what they are. And that happiness is a true reality. Very unfortunate on this plane that it is missed, for others seek that through their loins and through their womb and think that is love. That is a part of love, but that does not last. For that love chains itself, and from that, it causes bitterness.

How can one love another without possession, and without jealousy, and without insecurity, and without mistrust? Only when you have loved yourself beyond those measures—and this you will learn. And you will be able to look at the harshest and most wretched of entities and find God in them, like all messiahs do.

You will learn to love every entity, not as passion, not as clinging to, but you will learn to love him, for infinitely what he is, you are also. And what it is doing does not have conditions of favor any longer because judgment is removed. You are allowing them, through this process, the freedom that God gave them to enact, to be, to express, whatever way that was necessary to that evolvement. That is when you become God. That is when you are stripped of your fears; they do not exist. That is when you are stripped of your biases and your hypocrisy and your harsh judgments on those people you have just looked in the face.

Unconditional love, entity, is simply being love. That is all. When you are in love, entity, you can never hate. When you are in love and in the state of joy, you cannot find sadness. You know; you can look hard and cannot find it. And when you are in love, entity, you cannot find despair. And when you are in love, indeed, you can only find happiness.

When you learn to love you and look into the reflector and see the grand beauty that you are, and see the beautiful master you have become, and love all that you are—the ability to think, to contemplate, to design, to create—and learn to love that entity and to see you perfect in the now, that love, entity, will permeate itself into that which is termed divine joy. And divine joy can never see anything but divine joy in others, no matter how they express.

None can give unconditional love; they must become it. Live
it in your own life. Be unconditionally loving to you. Let
that be a light to others to spur them to go "within," to be
king to themselves, to find the beauty that they possess so
readily. Once they have experienced the love and the taste of
honey, they will want more of themselves, and will ask more
of themselves, and they themselves shall deliver more.

And the greater the love grows within you, the greater your kingdom shall manifest abundantly around you in this your reality. And the more it manifests, the more unlimited you will become.

Love, you are loved more than I can tell you. You have not created a word that fits this emotion. I love you because you are precious. You are the creators of the most beautiful flowers. You have created the most eminent of kingdoms! You have manifested mansions in your skies. You make your nest amongst the stars.
The God I teach you of loves you with greater love than you have ever fathomed. He is the ground that you walk on, the air that you breathe. He is the color of your skin, the magnificence in your eyes, the gentleness of your touch. He is the life that you are.

I am WISDOM

You have gained the value of the pearl this day in your time. You own it. This hour it is worthy to say, "Behold, I have gained the wisdom. I own it, this is my pearl."

Ｗith every irritation embraced
and loved and transformed, the transfiguration occurs, and your
soul becomes heavy-laden with the treasure of experience. Know you
why I say unto you that noble virtue is not the abstinence of life but the
embracing of it? For one who abstains from life has an empty soul.
One who is immersed in it dreams the illusions and the adventures and
grasps the wisdom; they are called the Gods of noble virtue. And unto
them and only them is the King of Kings, the Christ, availed unto. You
do not come back home empty-handed; you go back home rich with
treasure.

Whatever you feel you need to go through in order to gain your wisdom—or to get rid of your "blocks," as you term them to be—you do not have to. When you allow thoughts to flow through you like a wind, not judging them but allowing them, your soul will grasp firmly the emotions of allowing, and by doing so, it will be finished; it will be sent from your being and you will have lived one lifetime in that moment of allowance. Then you never have to be it, for you understand it, completely.

And all that has ever brought you happiness shall be wrapped up within the beauty of the pearl that lies within you. And then none shall have to teach you what you do with self thereafter; self declares that for itself. Then the Kingdom of Heaven and all of its majesty is made available to you.

Wisdom is a most wondrous treasure that belongs wholly to the spirit of man, which is collected within the soul of man. That is the only thing you take with you when you leave this plane. Think you take your wondrous linens with you? Think you take your mansions with you? Hmh? What think you take? You take what you are. That is what this whole life is about.

What I am teaching you here is that you have options and to be wise in the things which you confront every day in your experiences—for this one reason: the emotion that weighs on the soul determines your destiny; and if you do any one thing that wroughts guilt within your being, then the days that are beauteous, that are God, that are unfolding every moment, will be dull, hurtful, and insecure to you because you have guilt upon your being—and that is not worth it. I am teaching you to have your life the most splendid of all lives; and never be condemning of self but to love self every moment.

How you learn is by listening to you. And take from your language the thoughts of failure, guilt, fear, hurt; the thoughts of can't, will not, impossible and negative. When you remove all that, which is the mundaneness of mankind, you will find your splendid self. Then, when you listen to yourself in the mode of clarity, you will know the God within you.

Know also that you are responsible for your life; that you cannot take blame and put it at anyone else's kingdom, only at your own. And when you know that, then you shall assess unto your being that which brings forth the pearls of wisdom, indeed, the jewels of happiness.

Your creativity is a dream that you dream. And in the dream you go through the outrageous experiences of that dream, to contrive to give the Lord-God of your being the experience called wisdom—which is the only reality, because it is emotion; not confusion, but emotion. So out of the dream emerges wisdom.

Then when you listen to your thoughts, you will know that there is nothing greater than you. Then you will start making sense to you and your life, and for the first time in your existence, you will have answers that mean something, for they are coming from a sincere entity to a sincere entity: you to you.

The oyster is like you, except it learned from the beauty of life that every limitation, every hurt, every sorrow, every deception, every thing that irritates you, if you embrace it and love it, you own it, and the irritation becomes a pearl of wisdom.

I am KNOWINGNESS

I have come here, to bring you from your cloistered selves back into your "knowingness selves," and not with words that beseech the soul to humility and to "Godly acts," but with teachings that ring forth truth blatantly within the soul, that the soul urges itself to become the divine principle it forgot long, long ago.

Knowledge is like mist, "a great fog" as you would term it. It will come very thick and settle on the land and make everything like a dream. And lights will become diffused and flicker. And flowers will drip with the wetness of its immensity. And sounds are muted, and there is a great quiet that settles on everything. And some close it out and peer not into the mist, while a very few will walk into it to grasp its wonderland and how different it has changed the world. But when it rises and it leaves, perhaps a wisp will be left behind, or a very large drop from a leaf on an overhanging branch.

It is gone, but those which partake of wisdom, they keep forever within their beings what they have learned; those that have shut it out, they have never known or acknowledged the fog or the mist to have been.

Those that are endowed with a sincerity to know, you shall gain one hundred lifetimes in this lifetime alone for this effort that you have come forth this day. For those, that which I teach you will come sweetly unto your soul. And all that you felt to be truth, you will learn is—not through that which is termed dry philosophy, for that is boring and mundane. Not through that which is termed a "teaching"; that is meaningless—what is to gain in that? You are going to learn that what you have suspected to be truth will be manifested boldly for each of you that the discriminative eye and perhaps the weaker part of your being that wishes eagerly to explain everything away will now be convinced that your all-knowingness was right all along.

To know oneself is to have the quest for existence that goes on and on and on, for it will take that long to know who you are. You will never have a point of understanding that you can say, "Alas, this is who I am!," for in the next moment of consciousness, of being God, everything will have changed in will into the next moment of future.

We have brought the winds of change upon your plane. There is a great intelligence, supreme knowingness that waits above that which is called the restrictive shelf of consciousness here into an unlimited knowingness. You are part of it.

There is coming a great and wondrous day, very soon, that the knowledge of ages will be brought to this plane. And the scientific developments shall bloom as they have never bloomed before. And the wonderments of life will be unfolded through wondrous entities. But they will not give it to you; you will have to earn it! And the "earning" it is having the ability to perceive it.

I am OUTRAGEOUS

I am indeed outrageous…I am an enigma…I am confusing…but I work. I am not a spirit, I am an entity just like you.

It is not important who I am, it is important who you are. I already know who I am. So who be I is that which loves you greatly. Those who come to my audience do become and the wind is ever with them. They discover through this enigma who they are. That is why I am outrageous. Your part in this drama is to wake up from this dream into a vivid life that is manageable, controllable and desirable.

I am here in a wondrous disguise and I have chosen to come forth through this beloved woman who was once a child of mine long, long ago. I come forth without an image, imageless forever, to be that which you can touch, identify with, see as a contemporary person and hear a message that is not linked with worshipping anyone except yourself and that which is called the God within you.

This that I am has no image. There are no paintings, no statues, no monasteries, no churches or temples that you can come and worship and give your power away. I am imageless, because it is not for you to learn to worship me and become subservient and guilty, but that you have with you when you leave me no knowingness of Ramtha save the wind and what you feel and are inside. And that shall live forever and ever. You see, it is not that you worship some-one else, or an essence called God that is some-where in hyperspace, it is that God is that which you are, which lies latent within you. You are the Christ.

The Merv Griffin Show with guests JZ Knight and Ramtha, October 28, 1985

Merv: I would like to introduce to you JZ Knight.
(audience applauds enthusiastically)
Was Ramtha a philosopher 35,000 years ago?
What was he?
JZ: No, he was a warrior. He's the Ram that is the God of the Hindu people. He was a conqueror. He said he was driven to his enlightenment as a barbarian, through fear and hatred. Finally, by doing that all of his life, he came to a point where he began to contemplate what he was doing.
Merv: When Ramtha takes possession of your body and speaks through you, where is your consciousness?
JZ: Well, the Ram…actually does not take possession of my body. He comes around my body in the auric field and works through the seals or

chakras. I am what is called a pure channel because the whole of my essence goes to another time flow.

Merv: How much preparation do you need to call on your entity?

JZ: I don't call on him. It's a matter of me becoming aligned and becoming at peace and…not being nervous.

(JZ leaves her body, and slumps over. After a minute or so, the body comes to life and Ramtha is present.)

Merv: You're my first 35,000-year-old guest. Your home was Atlantis?

Ramtha: That was a place where I lived, but I was a pilgrim from a land called Mu (Lemuria).

Merv: What is your most important message that you want everyone on this planet to hear, to know? Is there one?

Ramtha: That what is termed God, which has been misunderstood, which has been taught to live outside of your being, is within your being. And that life is the grand experience where the kingdom of heaven is located, entity. And when you know you are God—that that which emanates within you is divine. You will find joy. Want? I do not want to deliver a message. I am that which I am. But for those who listen, the Christ within comes forward. You have lived seven and a half million years in search of paradise. But it has always been within you—never outside of you.

Merv: Ramtha, are we in danger of some great holocaust? Are we in danger on this planet of any major catastrophe?

Ramtha: It shan't ever be war that will destroy. That is not the great holocaust, entity. It is nature… diseasements. Indeed. That is already here, and yet it will grow even more vast. It is greater than any bomb that could have ever been dropped. Know you who created the disease? Mankind. For they have the power within them to do that—it is from their attitude.

Now, that is not a holocaust. They have done these things and manifested these things for a learning—to gain wisdom…the appreciation of life…the appreciation of what they call their enemies. They will learn through this to love their enemies. That is a grand teaching. The earth will never be destroyed. It will not rotate on its axis. And no one is going to drop bombs on it. It will go on and on. But the "greater consciousness" is coming.

Merv: I wonder if you have some joyful predictions for us for the next decade. We approach the year 2000 in less than fifteen years now. What can we look forward to?

Ramtha: What were you afraid you would see?

Merv: Oh, nothing. I'm wide open to accept whatever comes.

Ramtha: I know. It shan't come to pass what has been predicted for this plane. What will come to pass is the ceasing of a great disease and the offshoots of that disease. And as quickly as it came it will end. And yet the world and its consciousness will move into yet a greater understanding. This your country…you have a king that is a part of this country—his name is Reagan? He will help lead your government to a government likened to Solon's republic in a place called Greece. In that, he will give the country back to the people. That will occur, entity, before the end of this decade. Know you of entities that are in aeroships? You call them, ah—

Merv: Aliens.

Ramtha: Ah! But they are not aliens.

Merv: E.T.'s…extraterrestrials?

Ramtha: Indeed…humanity. They will become very much a part of your plane. That which is termed a new consciousness, it is coming forward. That which is called "the coming of Christ"—that will come before the end of this your time flow, your next decade.

Merv: The second coming of Christ?

Ramtha: But know you what that is? What think you that is?

Merv: The coming of Christ is when the son of God will come once again, as he did the first time.

Ramtha: But know you who the son of God is?

Merv: Do I know who he is? You mean he has an image
other than what we know?
Ramtha: The coming of Christ is the awakening of that
principle, of that divinity, in all people. 'Tis not one entity,
but the whole of the world, master, comes into that Christus,
into that understanding. That is what is meant by the
prophecy.
Merv: Will there be the two thousand years of brotherhood
that is predicted?
Ramtha: Two thousand years? Once superconsciousness has
been acclaimed here, it shan't end with two thousand years,
because your scientists will have conquered time and space.
Peace shall be an ongoing thing. War, entity, will die before
the end of the next decade.

Merv: Oh, that is good to hear. Thank you. Thank you for
coming, Ramtha.

JOY & HAPPINESS

I am

The greatest prayer you could ever say would be to laugh every day. For when you do, it elevates the vibratory frequency within your being such that you could heal your entire body.

The happiest of entities on this plane are those who do precisely what they want to do. The miserable ones here are the ones who try to make everyone else happy and do what they "should" do to appease for the sake of that which is termed notice, love, compassion and kindness.

Live for you. Do what you want to do. As long as you live for expectations of others, you will never be happy, and you will never lead, and you will never accomplish, nor will you ever be remembered.

You must do on this plane what makes you happy. There was not a great applause here when you were born. The whole of humanity did not turn out to witness your birth; only you and your mother. So why busy yourself living for the expectations and the reprisals of things that others think you "should" do when you could be living a happy life for the fulfillment of yourself and, much to your surprise, to the happiness of everyone else!

Happiness is the ability to be free of insecurities and worry and fear, to allow the self to create happily up here, in thought, that it unfolds out there. And if happiness is having a wafer for your dinner and cold water for your wine and the whole of the world for your home, so that you are not enslaved or entrapped to the envisionments of dogma and social pressures, well then, so be it.

Laughter is grand music to the soul and in a state of happiness you can achieve everything you desire. You can learn to transcend yourself beyond your illusions, beyond the fantasies of fashion and fad, society and judgment. For you are your greatest teacher. And the more you laugh and the more happy you feel, the closer you are to becoming God.

Happiness is not giving in to the demands and expectations of society, but rather doing what pleases your heart, your soul, your body. To be happy is to be yourself. Who could ever be happy by being the duplicate of someone else? There is no happiness in that, only mocked pleasure.

You are rich if you are happy in your soul, for gold cannot buy happiness. To perceive your treasure, look within to the love and beauty that is the unseen essence that you are.

Thus you must ascertain what it is about your being that you love and like…And what makes you unhappy or you dislike—you can master the change as it occurs in a moment. Of the realities that you have surrounded yourself with, that you look at every day in your time and the relation unto your soul makes you feel unhappy, get rid of them! If it is clothing, jewels, if it is a hovel, if it is entities—whatever it is, whatever you look at in association with, and it causes the memory of unhappiness or oppressiveness to occur, do away with it, entity.

It takes great strength and substance for an entity to do away with the things of unhappiness because he is throwing away his identity. You have kept these things and your moods and your temperaments because that is how you can equate that you are; that is what gives reality to yourself. If all, in a moment, they are thus thrust away from your being, then how can you identify yourself if it is not by objects, memories, personages, hovels? Then you are left rather bare, entity, but you are also left peaceful.

Decorate your walls with things of joy. Put upon your being those things that make you happy, regardless of what the world thinks of how you dress. And be unto yourself all things, careful to bring about that which is called joy, master. If you do this, you will elevate yourself into very much a level called peace, and there you can manifest the whole of the Kingdom of Heaven at your doorstep—because you have room to enjoy it.

Now, what is that called? Loving one's self. That, in its first steps, takes great strength to do, but it must be done; it is a necessity. Once you do that, you will become fulfilled within your being and you will have happiness in your being. And once you have obtained that, you will have a compassionate understanding of other people. Compassionate! You will allow them to do whatever they want to do because you realize it is a necessity for them to learn the things they are learning. And in that, when you pull away the restrictions, you can easily love another. Then, master, you love like God loves. Then you will be complete in this life and will have achieved what it takes entities eons to achieve, and it will be well spent.

And when moment by moment you give into that which is termed the love of self and allow that to bloom forth, the glory of the kingdom of Heaven will become prevalent before you.

Joy is the magic that allows it to occur. Those that are allowing the simpleness of joy to occur within their own beings are seeing life and its kingdom more than they have ever seen it before. And what they want is manifesting more than it has ever manifested before. And they are becoming youthful and vigorous in their entire beings because joy is prevalent in the God that they are.

Laughter is beyond words.

THE PATH IS WHERE YOU ARE.

The path is where you are. There is not a set path. Wherever you are is the right path. You are the way, the path and the light; that is a certainty.

Those who put the limitations upon man by saying that there is one road and there is one road only; and you must get on this road, for if you don't you will fail, they are the ones that put the thought of failure in the divine soul of man. And they are the ones that have invented the narrow road for the purpose of enslavement. It is easy to see that not all can fit on their road, for they have made it much too narrow!

But in that which is termed a soul understanding, the path to life and that which is called enlightenment is the feeling within; it is the Father within. And whatever you do, do it first by consulting yourself. If you do not feel happy about it, do not go, do not participate, do not enjoy. On the other hand, if it makes you feel happy, do so in zest and fulfillment and happiness.

The voice of God is that which urges, propels, directs you to where you are supposed to be and to do what you are supposed to do. This has often been referred to as "destiny." This voice is an emotion. It is also called that which is termed "the path of enlightenment."

To gain the path of enlightenment, as it were, you do not read, you do not follow; you listen to that subtle, small, noble voice that is called "feelings." And it is only through that voice that you can understand what to gain in your unlimited destiny, unlimited hope. That is the only way you will ever find it.

All people have their own path, their own truth—they are sovereigns in all of their paths. The one thing that they have in common, entity, is that they are advancing together; they are advancing into the same moments of the next moment. If you are wanting to know if you are on the right path, never pay any attention to who is on their path, for you can't be on theirs; you can only be on yours. And are you doing the right things, entity? Simply if you are doing it, you are on your own path and you are advancing like all are.

The road, it is a wondrous road. There is nothing on it to hurt you. But it does go at a good pace. And it does have a good widening about it. And all who walk on it advance. Go with the flow, abreast with the moments of God. Then, when you advance, you advance into foreverness, and the forever is where all will be in the eventuality of their beings.

Learn to listen to the feeling within you; it will never forsake you. Never! Go by the feelings that are in your uttermost being and let them be a lamp unto your night. They will always find your path right where you are.

When you listen to the God within you, you are living your life purposefully and in perfect alignment with the God within. It is that beauty, that covenant, that will light your path and your kingdom, and none other. When you learn to listen to you, you learn to listen to God; and when you learn to listen to God, then you become a part of the whole, the mass, and still retain your unique qualities of who you are this moment.

The path to God is an inward process and you began it when you came to this place. And when say you your story, the door opens. And as you go deeper in, and that journey I will go with you on, you'll begin to find that rather than a dark tunnel, a light will appear. It is called the light at the end of the tunnel. What does that mean, after all; do you think you will have to die to see that?

The light at every release of this dream becomes the reality; light and life are one and the same. That is the premise of reality. And the more of that light you begin to see, the greater the reality and the greater the Christ is exposed. That is the path that leads into superconsciousness.

I am LIGHT

You are the light of this plane,
whether you realize it or not. And
the light of this plane is freedom:
one that can exhibit the freedom of
the love of one's self to be lived for
the whole of the world and the
whole of humanity.

You have been prepared for eons, for teachings that were supreme; they have been carried in the soul all of this time. And alas, indeed, all of your journeys have only made you all the wiser. You were chosen to live your light to a world that has no ideal save in heroes in fiction and fantasy. And the light to live? Not as saviours but as the explicit God that you are taught that you are; brilliant, shining, mirthful, happy, and manifesting without doubt, indeed, and with courage because you simply are.

The key to the kingdom of heaven is locked within you. In the days to come in your time, we are going to reach beyond the illusions that lock and bind up the sacred soul, indeed the sacred light. And you are going to find that the "light fixtures" that surround your beings are going to transcend into different, brilliant colors, and become most visible.

An illumination occurs within the body which allows more knowingness to occur, that you are no longer a limited or a wretched creature of society or this plane; that you have, in fact, the ability to know of things predestined, preordained, of thought principle that no one else knows unless they too are unlimited like you are. You are going to become that which is termed the Lord God of your being.

It does not count in "heaven" how many entities you serve. What counts is how much you have served yourself, helped yourself, loved yourself, such that your communion with God is absolute. By being you, a unique sovereign entity, you serve the greatest purpose there is: you are a light to others.

If your light is such that the genuineness of its nature brings joy to but one entity in your life, you have made a grand difference; you have created worth. And if that joy be only unto you, it will have an aftermath in others.

The impulse of your electrum, or that which is termed your light, will be a spark unto others, and it will help them to become more unlimited.

It does not take one leader to create a light. It takes many learning of the light to become the same. In your days to come, you shan't need a leader. You and the whole rest of the world are only going to need the steadfast beauty, compassion, humbled strength, and profound wisdom that you possess to see through.

When you become who you are, you become what is called a "living light" to the world—to the world! Then, entity, peace walks upon this plane in sublime stature. Then you will have the capacity to live in freedom, to contemplate the vastness, unlimitedness. Then genius is born, a creative principle arises, the poet is born, the scribe arises, the wise man is seen.

There have been a few that have transcended the culture of limited consciousness, that have transcended limited thought, who have lived the God they are and have been bold enough to say that they are that. And they, entity, have changed the world simply by their presence.

There comes a greater civilization, not of humanity that is vulnerable, but of Gods that walk the earth again in brilliant reignment because the light does not come from without the being; it comes from within the being.

And never lose sight of that which is within, for in the days to come, entities, 'tis that "within" that the strength will be drawn from and the light will shine forth from.

All of you that are gathered here, I prepare for a splendid journey that will take you beyond this life into the next one, for I am a troubador, not only of inner space but of outer space. And for you who are attentive and love the Lord God of your being with all of your might, with all of your breath, with all of your life, when you leave this plane you shan't return here nigh for a long time, for there are journeys to go on just to awaken the memory within the divine self that it exists. Then when you return, you return as I have returned: unlimited, indeed, without judgment, indeed, with love that is the depth of all that is, and understanding, indeed, as no other. Then you can return as an entity reigning back into the original Godhead which you once were. This is already in the process and part of the reason I am here.

I am
LIFE

Live! Reach up unto your mountaintop and breathe the air and look into foreverness. Find a star that is elusive to you and ponder it. Become life. Be life. It is what all must eventually achieve and understand and where your wisdom and your teachings will be secured from. I will teach you how to live.

Go and ponder by a brook. Go and sit on top of a mountain. Go and sit in a field during a raging storm. Open your mouth and drink the rain. Get up before the sun and watch the splendor of the birthing sky. Watch the sky become rose and hues of gold, and watch the last relentless star lose favor to a greater light.

I want you to live! Does the rose remain the seed, hushed deep in the ground, and refuse to see the sun? No. Does the bee turn its face to the tempting flower and seek a weed? No. Does a man turn his eyes from a beautiful woman? No. Does the sun refuse to come up because the moon is still in the sky? And does the greatest star outshine the least of them? No. Why should you come out and see the things that exist in a simple coexistence? For then you will understand the Source, God, infinite Life!

There are those that go into caves, that go into temples and partake of learning and discipline themselves to be greater than life, to elude life, to hide from life, to calm their beautiful bodies, to restrict their loveliness and vision. But they will never know life unless they have been a participant in it.

'Tis not discipline or any ritualistic act that brings God into one's being. And it is not the abstinence of life either. It is living life to the fullest measure and finding the Father in every bloom, in every feather, in every laughter, in every embrace. Then you are called happy.

To life! With ruby red wine. Life is the only reality—
the only one. Everything else is an illusion upon its platform
and fades into the mists of yesterday or the unformed clouds of
tomorrow. You wanted to be here to live, because this is life.
Any other destiny is only a result of living.

Live for who you are and what you are and never deny the beauty of all that you are. When you express that which you be, express it, and do not ask what others think of it. Then you will have lived your truth blatantly. There is a saying that if you pass this life without having anybody talk about you, you've done something wrong. Be who you are, and let the world speak—then you will have notoriety at being yourself.

Once I was just like you, for that which you are I know to be a truth. This life is a conquest—a conquest of one's self. And that end is surrendering to the nobility that each self is. You will conquer that which does not allow you to see that, and being free of the altered self will allow you to be answerable to no one, have dominion over your kingdom, and above all—be free.

You, my esteemed beloved brethren, are more than that which is termed the creature of the flesh. You are awesome entities taking form to continue the creative ability that is within you. Without it, there is nothing. Without it, the value of thought does not propagate itself to become the next moment of life, or to become that which is termed the eternity that is yet to be lived.

In the eventuality, this plane will become a non-governing state. It can only be reached when each entity becomes aware that they are God and establishes within their own kingdom the sovereignty of self. And it can only be established by letting each live their truth. Man, in the depths of his being, worships freedom and respects it in others. When man is allowed to find the depths of his truth, he will express that sovereignness which will abolish government and give time, space, and measure back to contemplative conjecture and not reality.

And where, indeed, shall your eternity end? Nowhere. You are ongoing, entity. There is no end to it. When one learns that each moment one lives the refinement of his own opinionated self in becoming, then he becomes one day again the platform from which all life springs.

I prepare you for a splendid journey that will take you beyond this life into the next one, for I am a troubador, not only of inner space but of outer space. And for you who are attentive and love the Lord God of your being with all of your might, with all of your breath, with all of your life, when you leave this plane you shan't return here nigh for a long time, for there are journeys to go on just to awaken the memory within the divine self that it exists. Then when you return, you return as I have returned: unlimited, indeed, without judgment, indeed, with love that is the depth of all that is, and understanding, indeed, as no other. Then you can return as an entity reigning back into the original Godhead which you once were. This is already in the process and part of the reason I am here.

Many that come unto the audiences say unto me, "Ramtha, my beloved brethren, what be my purpose in this life? What is my destiny?" And I look at them and I say unto them, "To be happy, joyful."

Life, entity, is purposeful happiness. The illusions of creating that happiness are called purposeful destinies. I will tell you: Your greatest purpose is to live. To live! Living, entity, allows all happiness to occur…and all sadness, whatever your discretion be. Your greatest purpose is to live, to express the entity that you are, the embodiment of life.

You, who have made your transition unto this plane, it is a wondrous place. But whoever thinks that this is all has seen nothing! For greater kingdoms and adventures are there to come. Life is a splendid adventure! It is, indeed, a wondrous place to demonstrate the creative infiniteness of all that are gathered here; that is the purpose. When you create by developing thought into emotion, you create what is termed "reality." Reality is emotional life.

In this lifetime many of you are confused about what you are supposed to be. You are supposed to be you, without appeasing anyone else. And the one you trust is yourself, because you will never let yourself down. Allow your feelings to come forth and cherish what you are. Your body is your kingdom. It is the reflection of what you are inside, for you are known by your attitude, by your light. Love your body, keep it pure and keep it happy. It is what allows you to have the dreams. It is what allows you interaction with three-dimensional paradise. It is God.

When I say unto everyone that life is the only reality there is and that all of this is an illusion, worry is an illusion, fear is an illusion, I am speaking a most profound truth. For the only reality is feelings; everything else is a dream. And what you feel in the core of your being is what you are. Your life is a gift of God and you are held together by love. When you leave this plane, you advance beyond the senses of the body. And when you become God you get to take your body with you, wherever you go. Christ ceases the wheel of life and becomes the ongoing self.

There is no mystery to life. If you look around, you will see all the answers. If you listen to yourself and do what your self tells you to do, then you will soon find the manifestation of that doing. You are not the same as you were only moments ago, and you will not be the same in moments to come. For life is an ever-evolving consciousness that collects in its moment a totality of refinement, that allows you to bloom. It literally feeds you. And each moment you become grander, a greater entity to that which is called a total self, unto God the Father that blooms within your being. Thus, perfection can never be seen, for the Father and life are ever-changing every moment. You only are—nothing less and nothing more.

This your life is a wonderful spectacle. It should be reviewed in reverence, in holiness, divineness, for no matter who you are, you are always God. No matter the mask you wear, you are always God. No matter what relationship you are experiencing in this consciousness, you are still God. You, supreme creator, are creating your life right this moment by how you think.

Life is the grandest gift there is. It is not beholding to a past, or to an uncertain future. It is now. This moment is all there is…all there is. Life is a platform on which you, God of your being, have the reality to express and create on. And for what purpose, since you have been creating for eons in your time? For the express purpose of contemporary feeling; that is the reason.

To that which is this hour, I salute you, bless you, and share with you that which is termed, as it were, the ascension of yet another wondrous thing, the grape. For it has gone through the changes also. And it is heavy, heavy in its essence, it is impregnated with its perfume and is buoyant in its rubyness. But it is the fruit of the vine. The fruit of the vine which was once the seed, impregnated into the soil, the good earth, that was designed and the breath of life given to, by some great God. And we rejoice in it for it is the union of brother to brother, it is the union of seen and unseen, it is I Love You.

There will come an hour when your greatest lover is life.

Your lineages shall live on into a great age that I have spent nearly the whole of my existence in preparation for with other great entities to allow the beauty of mankind that is caught up in this wonderful flesh of his to exhibit a different thinking, a different attitude, a new life. And the tyrants and the warlords are being put under. And you, who are loved through and through by our beings, are going to learn what it is to live as Gods in utopia, for that is what has been prepared for you.

One day, you will sit on a plateau and the wind will blow through your hair, and you'll have a simple cloak on. And you will sit there and you will contemplate your life and you will realize the magnificent creature that you really are. And you will have not done one thing that would have ever harmed you or hurt you or would have disrespected you in any way, because, above all, it was your respect that you upheld and no one else's. That is when you can sleep and slumber at night and rejoice during the day and love what you are. Then you are a happy entity and, indeed, a happy God.

And there shall come a day when you will sit in the wind all alone and you will say, "Ramtha, my beloved brother, where be you amongst the stars? Have I learned enough? Have I strength enough? What is it you said? How can I remember? What did you tell me?" And you will rustle and bustle with yourselves. And finally, in desperation and feeling you have failed, the feeling will come to you and you will know, for what I have taught you has not been words; they have been meanings, complete memory, an emotion that is there everlasting, forever. And when the feeling arises, you will come down from the mountain, and the wind will be nigh at your back, and the exuberance of life will be in you and in your veins as it was in mine. And behold, the prophecy of the great meek, the great humbled strength, the light of the world will be upon the land.

THE CHANNEL

My name is JZ Knight and I was the first person to create this body. It has belonged to me for many years now, I lease it out every once in a while.

The process started back in 1977 with Ramtha's appearance to me in my life—which blew me away, because I had never even imagined that such things existed, but nonetheless, the process itself is basically history at this point. To many people it is a phenomenon that…either it is, or it isn't—there's no explanation point. And it is a very difficult thing to understand—this enigma.

So the enigma of allowing this to happen is because when I was a little girl, the one entity that I loved in my life that was constant was God the Father—I always loved God. I didn't have a fairy godmother, I had God, who lived in the clouds, and I loved this entity, and I didn't know why. I talked to God, the wind, and I always knew when he answered me because the wind always came up. Well, I always said that I wanted to do something grand, so what does a small person, who doesn't have much—what can you offer to God, when He's got everything? So I said, I want to be able to do something one of these days that whatever it is, I want to make a contribution. And I forgot about that and that was when I was a young woman, as a teenager, and it wasn't until I had my children, it wasn't until I was in the most settled, mundane social conscious life that this entity totally upturned my whole life. Well, guess what—God took me up on my

deal. Except I wouldn't come to realize it until this last year, who the God was that I was really talking to. Ramtha listened—he was my father in another lifetime, but it was the God within me that heard then, and kept that conviction. And allowed the flow to come about.

People say, "How many years have you been in metaphysics?" and I say None. They say, "Well, you know you're a psychic" and I say, No, I don't know I'm a psychic. I don't even know what that means. I had no preparation at all. This entity came into my life and turned my life totally upside down. My grandfather clock which was my prize possession, Ramtha got mad at one day because it was "binging" and he was talking to me and it's never worked since. It still doesn't work.

Well, I used to tell people all the time, I don't really know why Ramtha picked me, I didn't have a lot on the ball. I didn't know about ectoplasm, I certainly didn't know about planes. I didn't understand levels, I didn't understand ALLOW—I thought that if somebody punched you in the nose, you get 'em back. I didn't understand that you weren't supposed to do those things. So, I would always tell people, "well, I don't know," and I was almost apologizing because I was the channel. Do you know why I was doing that? Because I didn't love myself.

You know, I had Ramtha in my life on a conscious level since 1977 and it wasn't until this year (1985) that I got it together

with this master because I fought him all of the way, I griped and bitched at him a lot, I felt imposed upon, I felt like my life wasn't my life any longer. Days out of my life—I had no recollection of them.

Only until this year have I found out, through all of the fire, through confronting all of the fears. (You think you have fears? I have a closet full of them!) And one by one I had to face those fears—whether it was through my family, my children, my friends, the fear of somebody thinking I was weird because I was a channel, the fear of somebody finding out about it. Did you know that the *National Enquirer* did an article about Shirley MacLaine and me? You know, I was so petrified that the children would get harangued at school, that my entire staff went out early in the morning and bought up all of the National Enquirers before they ever hit the Yelm drugstore. Yelm was uninformed by the *National Enquirer* that week. And we all went "whew!" I'm sure glad we slid through that one! Afraid of everything. Afraid that I'm too young to grow old. You know, you should check out my face some-time when the Ram's finished with it, just check it out! You know women try to smile, but they try not to smile too much so that they don't get wrinkles, so they change their smile. When Ramtha finishes with my face, I have wrinkles from here to here and you can see where the impression of that beautiful face once was. All I have to do is look in the mirror when I get back into my body. You know, there's so much happiness on my face, it makes me sad.

There were times that I did not ever want to see the Ram again, and there were times that I never wanted to do this again because no one was getting it, including me. And I just couldn't handle it a lot of the times. So I would say, why can't you lay off the fears and bring something else like a new dishwasher or something jazzy like that. And he would send something like that along. But you know how long your happiness lasts when you get it? It lasts only until you have to clean it up for the first time. Then it's sort of over with after that.

Some of you have this illusion about me, that because I am the channel for Ramtha, that I am sort of an elite individual, that's excluded from the fire, from the judgment, from the lack of love, the lack of self respect. You think that somehow because I'm Ramtha's channel that that doesn't exist in my life—that I go back to the ranch and live in a utopia of Arabian horses and sunny days. That's not how it is.

Every time the Ram delivered a teaching that involved a manifestation, or sent all of your fears to your door, I got all of those when I went home. I still go through this process, and everything that everyone receives, I also receive, sometimes one hundred times worse, because I have blotches of my life that I can't recreate, they are gone forever, my life was waking and going to sleep, waking and going to sleep.

The enigma process is, I am not a trans-medium, I am a channel. There is a difference. A person who is a trans-medium subdues their alter-ego self and can hear another entity and spirit move into their auric field; they give you the information third-hand.

I leave my body. Every time that I go away—I die. It's just exactly what you do when you pass this plane and I go to a great space in a different time in a different understanding,

far from this reality. And yet when I come back, it's like a moment later, except when I started it was daylight and now it's nighttime.

Someone asked me, "JZ, do you want to be a teacher?" and I sat there for a few minutes, and I said, "No, I don't want to be a teacher." And he said, "Why wouldn't you want to be a teacher?" And I looked at him and said, "I am not qualified to be one." That was sort of a mystery...not qualified to be one, because you see where I am at now is in a space to allow.

Allow, because I've allowed me to be that way. I will leave the teaching to someone who knows how to handle it, who knows how to make it happen, who is well equipped to do that.

But for me personally, I've built this house that was in my dreams all of my life.

I want to go back home and get into my kitchen. I love to cook. I want to go back home and see my two sons when they come home from their school. I want to put my arms around my husband and I want to smell his hair and I want to plant my flowers in the spring. That's what I want because it is my life and that is what makes me happy.

I'll leave the other part to the Ram because he is the one who evokes glory within us individually. I could never do that—don't want to. I just want to be me. That's what makes me happy.

Not again in my life will I do anything that goes outside of that understanding. I never will again give away my power. I never will again pull the rug out from under myself, because inside of me I don't think I'm worth it. I'll always love me. And if what makes me happy is living under a tent while it is raining or cooking a pot of beans on an open fire, then I'll do that. And I'll live through all of my joys until I own them and, then, I'll go on to something more joyful. I move in that sort of understanding.

And if the world criticizes me for this or for that, it is OK, because I don't hold a grudge or anger. I allow them, just like I allowed my children. I've learned that valuable truth.

I don't desire to be famous. I was famous in another life and still died a lonely woman. It doesn't make any difference if the world worships you, you can still be lonesome. I don't desire that. I desire that what I've learned and the privilege of having the Ram in my life be made available to people. Because I love God. I love the essence called Is. All of my

easy, I don't know. But whatever it takes, it is worth it. It is worth it, because then you are not afraid to live, you are not afraid to express.

I am not your Guru. I won't be your teacher, I just want to be me.

Build your own dreams. Have your own holy place, wherever that is, but make it yours. Please, don't put on my shoulders the responsibility of your happiness because it doesn't belong there. Create your own paradise. If it starts out with a little place and goes to a big place, it is OK as long as it makes you happy. Listen to your knowingness and listen to your joy.

life, I have loved that.

I have come a long way from being a socially acceptable woman, who was very naive, to someone who is no longer afraid, because I owned the truth and I owned me. The secret was to go through it, to take the steps that society said you should never do. I did it anyway because it was right for me, it was my own truth.

There are no differences between any of us. It was really hard for me to understand. Maybe for some of you it will be

I love you from the Lord God of my being and for the God, the Is that is my life. May peace and harmony follow you in the days to come.

I love you.

PHOTOGRAPHER'S NOTES

Cover: Seattle Past Lives Intensive, May 1985, during a break.

Introduction: San Diego Intensive, May 1985, teaching.

Estes Park, Colorado, retreat, September 1985, JZ Knight and Anne-Marie Bennstrom.

Yucca Valley, California, retreat, March 1985, Ramtha with Anne-Marie Bennstrom, after greeting the sun.

Who Be I: Estes Park, Colorado, retreat, September 1985, teaching.

Nature: Yucca Valley, California, retreat, May 1985, Ramtha greeting the sunrise.

Yucca Valley, California, retreat, March 1985, Ramtha waiting for sunrise, watching the moon.

Yucca Valley, California, retreat, March 1985, Ramtha teaching in the desert.

Noble Virtue: Estes Park, Colorado, retreat, September 1985, children's hour. Ramtha met with children alone for a few hours.

Estes Park, Colorado, retreat, September 1985, pearl ceremony.

The Teacher: San Diego Intensive, May 1985, during a break.

San Mateo Intensive, September 1985, teaching (Ramtha in blue).

Seattle Intensive, April 1985, past life reflections.

Yucca Valley, California, retreat, March 1985, Ramtha teaching in the desert.

Seattle Intensive on Soulmates, November 1985, Ramtha walking through the audience.

Becoming: San Diego Intensive, May 1985, process of aligning the body, before the wine ceremony.

Peeling: New York City Intensive, August 1985, wine ceremony.

Unconditional Love: San Mateo Intensive, September 1985, wine ceremony.

Estes Park, Colorado, retreat, September 1985, sitting by the river.

Wisdom: San Mateo Intensive, September 1985, Ramtha speaking with a couple.

Estes Park, Colorado, retreat, September 1985, pearl ceremony.

Knowingness: San Diego Intensive, May 1985, Ramtha raising the energy in JZ's body during a moment of contemplation.

Outrageous: San Mateo Intensive, September 1985, Ramtha coming into the body.

The Merv Griffin Show, October 28, 1985, with JZ Knight.

The Merv Griffin Show, October 28, 1985, with Ramtha.

Joy and Happiness: San Diego Intensive, May 1985, a moment of joy.

Seattle Intensive on Soulmates, November 1985, Ramtha laughing with Anne-Marie Bennstrom.

The Path: Estes Park, Colorado, retreat, September 1985, Ramtha teaching during pearl ceremony.

Light: Yucca Valley, California, retreat, September 1985, a back room.

Life: Estes Park, Colorado, retreat, September 1985, water toast.

The Channel: Seattle Intensive on Soulmates, November 1985, wine toast.

Yucca Valley, California, retreat, March 1985, closing celebration.

Seattle Intensive on Soulmates, November 1985, wine toast.

Yucca Valley, California, retreat, March 1985, surprise birthday party for JZ Knight.

Albuquerque, New Mexico, U.S. National Arabian Horse Show, October 1985, son Chris won championship in his class. Left to right: JZ, Chris, Jeff Knight, JZ's mother.

Albuquerque, New Mexico, U.S. National Arabian Horse Show, October 1985. JZ and husband Jeff with winning horse, Sterling.

Estes Park, Colorado, retreat, September 1985. JZ Knight at opening night party.

Albuquerque, New Mexico, U.S. National Arabian Horse Show, October 1985. JZ Knight with husband Jeff and a friend.

Albuquerque, New Mexico, U.S. National Arabian Horse Show, October 1985. Jeff and JZ Knight cheering for their son who had just won championship in his class.

PUBLISHER'S ACKNOWLEDGEMENTS

The publishers would like to express their deepest appreciation to all who have helped in the creation of this book: Nubar Alexanian for his superb photography; JZ Knight and Anne-Marie Bennstrom for contributing their writing and energy; Dr. Steven Weinberg for helping to create and edit the Ramtha text, and Sue Fazio and Carol Wright for graciously sharing additional Ramtha material; Paul Berry for his counsel and editing; Karenina Griswold, Pat Jacobs, Elizabeth Martin and Goodie Moeschl and all the Ramtha staff for their love and support; Steven Bakker, Rebecca Koch and Jean Wright for their editorial assistance; Kathy Woody and Linda Kopetzky for unselfishly giving their time; Daniel and Michaela Belding for their steadfast commitment to bringing this dream to fruition; and Bob Goodman and Les Sinclair for providing technical assistance in the publishing of this book.

Sovereignty Inc. Publishers
P.O. Box 909
East Sound, Washington 98245
206-376-2177

Title: RAMTHA $19.95 hardbound

Masterworks, Inc.
P.O. Box 1847
Friday Harbor, Washington 98250
1-800-445-1313

Title: VOYAGE TO THE NEW WORLD
$9.95 softcover

For more information about ongoing
events or the Ramtha Dialogue audio and
video cassettes, please write to:

Ramtha Dialogues®
P.O. Box 1210
Yelm, Washington 98597

OTHER BOOKS FROM BEYOND WORDS PUBLISHING

Within a Rainbowed Sea, by Christopher Newbert
"We are kin to the stars, part of a universal family, and Within a Rainbowed Sea is about that connection. It is a visual poem, photographs and words celebrating not just the intricate fabric of life which evolution has woven in the sea, but the origin and life force common to all things."
A spectacular look at the world's most acclaimed collection of underwater images, featuring more than 158 close-up full color photographs plus an evocative text. A sensual, artistic and compelling book highly recommended as both a science and art piece. Winner best printed book of the year, Printing Industries of America.

A 13 month calendar containing 26 full color photographs from the national award winning book "Within a Rainbowed Sea." It offers ample space for personal notations, lists phases of the moon, and full moon times and all national US and Canadian holidays. Special features include: 9 color reproductions and two pages of informative text.

Molokai an Island in Time, by Richard Cooke III
Molokai an Island in Time: An American photographer's twenty two year adventure discovering the heritage and beauty of Hawaii. 156 vivid color plates depict striking natural scenery of Molokai and her people. National award winning design and superb print quality make this book an invaluable addition to every home or office.
Merit award winner for book design, Art Directors Club of New York.

For further information about these award winning publications write or call
BEYOND WORDS PUBLISHING
P.O. Box 2097
Portland, OR 97208-2097
(503) 228-0910
and a free catalogue will be sent to you immediately.

Jan